# ESSENTIAL
# KITCHENS

# TERENCE
# CONRAN
# ESSENTIAL
# KITCHENS

**THE BACK TO BASICS GUIDE TO HOME DESIGN, DECORATION & FURNISHING**

conran
OCTOPUS

# Contents

14

# Planning & Layout

# INTRODUCTION

## PLANNING &

## LAYOUT

## FIXTURES &

## FITTINGS

## DECOR & DETAIL

# Introduction

Kitchens today perform many roles beyond the obvious. Increasingly, we are as likely to eat in them as cook in them. They are where friends and family gather, children play and do their homework, and household chores are carried out. In many ways, they are the heart of the home, the backdrop to everyday living.

As kitchens have shifted to centre stage, there has been a knock-on effect on the way our homes are planned as a whole. The separate kitchen, devoted exclusively to the preparation and cooking of food behind a closed door, is becoming a rarity these days. Much more common are kitchens that double as eating places or kitchens that are fitted into part of a multipurpose living space. While this is not to say that kitchens have necessarily become bigger, they have certainly become more open and inclusive. Where possible, many people also prefer to arrange their kitchens with a connection to outside space.

The concept of the kitchen as a living space is relatively new. In the era of domestic service, the kitchen was a 'below stairs' domain hidden from public view, judged solely on the merits of the food that came out of it. The dream kitchens of the immediate postwar period were temples of technical efficiency, where melamine worktops and labour-saving appliances promised to take the drudgery out of housework and the preparation of meals, activities that were performed more or less exclusively by women.

During the 1960s and 1970s, when people started eating in their kitchens and even entertaining in them, a greater emphasis was placed on style: country-style kitchens in the city, period-style kitchens in new homes, Mediterranean-style kitchens a long way from the sea. Over the ensuing decades, kitchens increasingly have come to be seen as status symbols, even in households where cooking is fairly perfunctory. Most recently the restaurant kitchen has become the role model for kitchen design, inspired by cookery programmes and the popularity of dining out. Fitted with sleek stainless steel and equipped with hard-core gadgetry, for some the professional kitchen is the ultimate domestic trophy.

LEFT: SIMPLE DETAILING AND THE USE OF TACTILE NATURAL MATERIALS BRING AN ELEMENTAL QUALITY TO A CONTEMPORARY VERSION OF A COUNTRY KITCHEN.

ABOVE: PLACING A SIMPLE, INEXPENSIVE TABLE AND CHAIRS IN A SMALLER KITCHEN CREATES A CONVENIENT AND STYLISH EATING AREA.

continued

# Introduction

Now that we spend more time in the kitchen doing things other than cooking, there is an increased recognition that its design should support and reflect the way we live. This does not mean that style has to take a back seat, rather that creating a welcoming space tailored to our lifestyles as well as our tastes should take precedence over superficial design statements.

If the kitchen is the heart of the home, at the heart of every kitchen is food – preparing and cooking it, enjoying and sharing it. Sitting down to eat together is more than refuelling, it is the glue of family life. You can do many things virtually these days – communicate, shop, play games, have a conference – but the kitchen is often the place where real life happens.

Big or small, fitted or unfitted, all kitchens must work well. This means getting the layout right, properly integrating servicing with appliances and providing adequate space for food preparation and storage, along with many other practical and aesthetic considerations. Kitchens, aside from their roles as living spaces, see intensive use on a daily basis and any shortfalls in efficiency will be acutely felt. Contrary to what many kitchen manufacturers might have you believe, you do not need to spend a fortune to create a successful and stylish cooking and dining space. What it does take is intelligent planning: if the layout and servicing function well, whatever style you choose will automatically reflect this integrity.

ABOVE: A SLEEK L-SHAPED KITCHEN FORMS THE HUB OF AN INCLUSIVE MULTIPURPOSE SPACE WHERE COOKING IS A CENTRAL FAMILY ACTIVITY.

RIGHT: SUCCESSFUL KITCHENS ARE ALL ABOUT GOOD SYSTEMS OF ORGANIZATION. HERE, FITTED UNITS ARE COMBINED WITH A UTENSIL RAIL AND SHELVING.

INTRODUCTION

# PLANNING &
# LAYOUT

FIXTURES &

FITTINGS

DECOR & DETAIL

# Assessing your needs

When planning your kitchen you must first assess your priorities and take a critical look at the space at your disposal.

- Who uses the kitchen?
- Do you cook on a regular basis or only rarely?
- What type of cooking do you do?
- What activities take place in the kitchen? Are there other functions you would like to accommodate?
- Do you eat in the kitchen?
- Is your present kitchen big enough for your needs or is it feasible to extend it?
- Is your kitchen located in the right place or could it be moved to a different part of your home? How accessible is it to the main entrance or to outdoor areas?
- Could servicing be improved? Are there enough power points for example?
- Does your kitchen receive plenty of natural light? If not, could existing openings be enlarged to provide better illumination?
- Think about your storage requirements. Do you buy in bulk?
- Which kitchen appliances do you need? Do you need to accommodate laundry appliances in the kitchen or could they be moved elsewhere?
- Think about the types of kitchen you prefer: fitted, unfitted or a combination of both?
- Which kitchen items do you wish to see on display, if any?
- What is your budget?

ABOVE: ISLAND LAYOUTS ALLOW YOU TO SOCIALIZE AS YOU PREPARE AND COOK FOOD, BUT THEY DO REQUIRE A GENEROUS AMOUNT OF FLOOR AREA.

RIGHT: MANY PEOPLE PREFER TO SITE THEIR KITCHENS WHERE THERE IS EASY ACCESS TO OUTDOOR SPACES.

# Levels of change

How much time and money you decide to spend on your kitchen will depend on factors such as your budget and the length of time you expect to stay in your home.

## Facelift

Cosmetic changes can give a tired kitchen a facelift for a relatively small amount of money and effort. This is a good option if you are renting, if your existing kitchen is already well planned, or if you do not expect to stay in your present home for very long. Changes include:

- Redecoration: repainting, retiling, reflooring
- Installing a new worktop
- Replacing cupboard doors, drawer fronts and handles
- Improving lighting

## Refit

If you are prepared to make more extensive changes, you can upgrade key parts of your kitchen or rip it out entirely and start again. Changes include:

- Installing new units or freestanding furniture
- Upgrading appliances
- Reworking the layout
- Changes to servicing: moving radiators, installing new power points

## Structural work

At the top end of the scale, changes that involve structural work are generally more expensive and require professional input. Changes include:

- Extending your kitchen, either to the side or the rear
- Removing partition walls
- Enlarging openings: making windows bigger or installing glazed doors
- Moving your kitchen to a new location and creating new service connections

LEFT: THE GROUND FLOOR OF A TERRACED HOUSE HAS BEEN EXTENDED INTO THE SIDE RETURN TO CREATE A SPACIOUS KITCHEN AND TOP-LIT EATING AREA.

RIGHT: KITCHENS DO NOT HAVE TO BE EXPENSIVE TO BE WORKABLE; USING SALVAGED AND RECLAIMED MATERIALS IS A GOOD WAY OF CUTTING COSTS.

# Professional help

The scale of your plans will determine whether or not you need professional help and, if so, of what type. Do not be tempted to take on work yourself simply to save money – assembling a flat-pack kitchen is not for the faint hearted.

Make sure that whoever you employ has the right accreditations. Always ask to see examples of previous work and take up references. It is important to get everything in writing: the full specification, cost breakdown and schedule.

### Design professionals
- For large projects, particularly those that entail structural changes or where permissions may be required, it is best to seek advice from a design professional such as an architect or an interior designer, at least for the initial stages.
- In-house designers, either at specialist suppliers or major retailers, can help you refit an existing kitchen.
- If structural alterations or major changes to servicing are required, you may need advice from a surveyor.

### Contractors & installers
- For major remodelling, you will need to hire a firm of reputable builders to carry out the construction work.
- Many kitchen specialists or retailers have their own installers.
- New service connections need to be carried out by qualified electricians, plumbers or the relevant utility.
- Custom results can be achieved by commissioning a bespoke design from a cabinetmaker.

ABOVE: A SEAMLESS PANEL LIFTS UP TO REVEAL HIDDEN STORAGE. FITTED KITCHEN SUPPLIERS SPECIALIZE IN THIS TYPE OF DETAILING.

RIGHT: A PROFESSIONAL-STYLE DOUBLE RANGE FORMS THE CENTREPIECE OF A BESPOKE KITCHEN. THE ISLAND UNIT HAS BEEN EXTENDED AROUND THE PILLAR TO MAKE MAXIMUM USE OF THE SPACE.

# Budgeting & buying

A new kitchen is a substantial investment. Before you finalize your plans, work out what you can realistically afford. The overall figure should include five to ten per cent as a contingency allowance should anything go wrong during the course of the installation. In addition to units, appliances, fittings and fixtures, your budget may also have to cover professional fees, a fee for the initial consultation and kitchen plan, demolition and removal, and delivery and installation, depending on the scope of the work.

Whether you buy a kitchen from a mass-market retailer, specialist supplier or custom kitchen designer, your budget and your list of priorities will form the basis of initial discussions. If you cannot afford everything you want, a good consultant or designer should be able to suggest alternatives, such as a less expensive worktop or a cheaper type of flooring.

### Points to consider

- Large retailers generally do not offer site visits, which means that you will have to provide accurate measurements yourself.
- You may be required to provide a deposit of about 25 per cent. Watch out for expensive cancellation clauses.
- Find out if the company provides written guarantees against faulty fittings, appliances and installation.
- Get a detailed written quotation that covers every aspect of the job, and an estimate in writing of how long it will take.

ABOVE: A COUNTRY-STYLE KITCHEN HAS BEEN CUSTOM MADE FROM A RECLAIMED CUPBOARD AND SINK. WICKER BASKETS AND RETRO KITCHEN EQUIPMENT COMPLETE THE RUSTIC LOOK.

LEFT: SYMMETRICAL WHITE CUPBOARDS CREATE A CONTEMPORARY DESIGN FEATURE. A BESPOKE KITCHEN CAN BE BUILT TO REFLECT YOUR PERSONAL STYLE AND FULLY EXPLOIT THE SPACE AT YOUR DISPOSAL.

# Ergonomics

Ergonomics is the study of the relationship between workers and their environment. Successful ergonomic design should reduce discomfort and prevent injury. The key concept of kitchen planning is the 'work triangle'. Ergonomic studies have shown that the distances between the sink, refrigerator and cooker should not be too great in order to maximize efficiency and safety.

- Ideally, an imaginary line drawn between the three key areas of activity should not exceed 6m (20ft). At the same time, at least 900mm (35in) is needed between each work zone for ease of movement and to allow appliance doors to open.
- Plumbing is disruptive and expensive to change, so it is a good idea to start with the current location of the sink and plan the layout from there. Try not to interrupt the flow of the work triangle with tall units.
- Kitchen cabinetry and many appliances come in a range of standard dimensions, which allows for easy integration. A modular size of 600mm (24in) wide by 600mm deep is common for base units, while the standard elbow height of fitted units is 900mm (35in). Shallower, taller and narrower units are also available to help you make the most of the space at your disposal.
- Plan the layout to minimize bending down and reaching up. Large, heavy items should be kept low down, preferably in deep drawers that slide out for easy access.

ABOVE: DEEP UNIT DRAWERS PROVIDE CAPACIOUS STORAGE FOR CROCKERY. MANY DRAWERS HAVE A 'SOFT-CLOSE' MECHANISM THAT PREVENTS THE CONTENTS FROM BEING JARRED.

RIGHT: HANGING KITCHEN UTENSILS ABOVE THE HOB MAKES THEM EASY TO REACH DURING COOKING.

# Types of layout

Kitchen efficiency does not depend on the size or shape of the space at your disposal: it is down to good planning. Each of these six types of layout is based around the principle of the 'work triangle' and will result in a practical, hard-working kitchen.

## Single-line

- A simple layout that is good for narrow rooms or for a kitchen that forms part of an open-plan space.
- Suitable for two people to use at once.
- Ideally requires 3m (10ft) of uninterrupted wall space.
- The longest stretch of worktop should be between the oven and sink.
- Requires built-in or built-under appliances.
- Can be screened with sliding or folding doors to hide from view.

## Galley

- A practical, efficient layout that is good for small or narrow spaces. Worktops are arranged on both sides of the room, facing each other.
- If the layout is very compact, this is essentially a one-person kitchen.
- Ideally requires at least 1.2m (4ft) of space between facing units.

## L-shaped

- A versatile layout for kitchens that are integrated with living or eating areas. Cupboards are usually arranged along two adjacent walls.
- Hob, refrigerator and sink should be separated by lengths of worktop to provide enough preparation space.
- Carousel units can be used in the corner to exploit all available space.

## U-shaped

- An adaptable layout that suits both large and small spaces. Appliances and units are fitted on three full walls.
- Maximizes preparation area and storage space.
- More than one person can work effectively at the same time.
- For small U-shaped layouts, ensure there is at least 2m (6½ft) in the middle.
- For long, thin spaces or large kitchens, arrange the layout so that the work triangle is at the bottom of the U to keep distances manageable.

LEFT: THE STREAMLINED DESIGN OF A SINGLE-LINE KITCHEN ALLOWS EASY ACCESS TO AN EATING AREA BEYOND. KITCHEN EQUIPMENT IS STOWED AWAY TIDILY IN TALL FITTED CUPBOARDS.

continued

# Types of layout

### Island

- A generous, open layout that is suitable only for larger spaces. A central island within an L-shaped or U-shaped layout creates a separate working area around which people can gather.
- The hospitable and inclusive layout allows the cook to remain in touch with guests. Good for open-plan kitchen/eating areas.
- The work triangle should be arranged so that needless journeys do not have to be made around the island.
- Islands can be used to house a hob or sink. Plumbing and electrical connections will need to be routed under the floor.
- Simpler islands provide storage and extra preparation space.

### Peninsula

- A variant on the L-shaped or U-shaped layout, the peninsula kitchen includes a worktop that juts out.
- A peninsula is a good way of incorporating a compact kitchen area within an open-plan living space.
- The peninsula can serve as a breakfast bar or counter on one side and help to screen kitchen activity from view. It can also accommodate one of the three main activity zones.

ABOVE: A SMALL PENINSULA WORKTOP DOUBLES UP AS A NEAT BREAKFAST BAR FOR TWO PEOPLE.

RIGHT: AN EXPANSIVE STONE ISLAND UNIT COMBINES AN INSET SINK, LARGE WORKTOP AND SUBSTANTIAL BAR AREA FOR EATING.

# Fitted or unfitted

Regardless of whichever kitchen layout you opt for, you have a further choice to make: whether to go the fitted or unfitted route. Back in the 1950s the fully fitted kitchen was a status symbol and today it remains by far the most popular option. Contemporary modular designs, featuring freestanding elements, have recently updated the unfitted look and broadened its appeal. In reality, many kitchens contain both fitted and unfitted elements.

If you do not have very much space at your disposal, a fitted kitchen is the best option. With good planning, every last bit of space can be put to use. Fitted kitchens are also visually neater, which helps if your kitchen forms part of an open-plan area. They cannot be achieved piecemeal, however, and you cannot take them with you if you move to another home.

The unfitted kitchen once relied heavily on traditional freestanding pieces such as dressers and butcher's block tables. With the rise in popularity of statement appliances such as retro-style refrigerators and range cookers, there has come a new trend for modular units that house fittings and fixtures in stand-alone elements. Some designs have a distinctly professional edge. The advantage of this approach is that you can acquire elements as your budget allows and be reasonably flexible with arrangement.

ABOVE: A COUNTRY-STYLE BUTCHER'S BLOCK ON CASTORS IS SLOTTED INTO A RECESS TO PROVIDE STORAGE WITH A RUSTIC FEEL.

LEFT: DARK WOOD UNIT FRONTS AND PANELS MAKE A STRONG CONTEMPORARY STATEMENT. RECESSED DOWNLIGHTS AT THE BASE OF THE WALL CABINETS HIGHLIGHT THE WORKTOP.

# Design approaches

Good organization is the foundation of all successful kitchens, but kitchens should also reflect how you live and the preferences you express elsewhere in your home. If the kitchen is the natural setting for the type of food you like to cook, equally importantly, it should be a place where you enjoy spending time.

An eternally popular design approach is the country kitchen with its warm, relaxed simplicity. Natural robust materials and classic features such as deep Belfast sinks, dressers and butcher's block tables evoke an appealing back-to-basics quality. Country kitchens at their best are large, unfitted generous spaces – the fitted 'country' kitchen with its reproduction detailing always looks a little bogus. Variations on the theme take inspiration from farther afield. If you particularly enjoy cooking and eating Eastern food, for example, there is no reason why your kitchen should not reflect this in its design and appearance.

At the opposite end of the spectrum is the professional kitchen. Sleek stainless steel surfaces and fittings, a gleaming array of equipment and utensils, and a no-nonsense approach to décor announce the domain of the serious cook. Paradoxically, a small kitchen fitted out for maximum efficiency can also be very appropriate for those with refined culinary skills.

ABOVE: STAINLESS STEEL SURFACES ARE A HALLMARK OF THE CONTEMPORARY PROFESSIONAL KITCHEN. THEY DO, HOWEVER, REQUIRE ADDITIONAL MAINTENANCE.

RIGHT: A COUNTRY AESTHETIC IS SPELLED OUT IN A COMBINATION OF OPEN SHELVES AND CUBBYHOLES FILLED WITH WICKERWORK CONTAINERS.

# Inclusive kitchens

The inclusive kitchen, embracing a range of activities that may have little to do with cooking, has become increasingly popular in recent years. This flexible pattern includes kitchen-diners, multipurpose spaces that have kitchens slotted into them, and family kitchens where everyone mucks in together.

The central principle of this approach is a generosity of spirit. While the actual kitchen area may be tightly planned and well organized, the open nature of the layout maintains an overall sense of expansiveness. At the very least, the inclusive kitchen provides somewhere where people can sit down, eat and talk together – the days of the separate formal dining room are surely numbered.

What the inclusive kitchen should not include is unnecessary clutter. If your kitchen is also the household nerve centre keep ahead of the game by providing dedicated storage areas for routine paperwork. Cupboards, lidded boxes, storage caches under window seats or built-in banquettes can make good stowing places for toys, games and any other paraphernalia that supports family activities.

When children are small and underfoot, pay special attention to kitchen safety. Keep flexes out of reach, turn pan handles away from the edge of the cooker and fit locks to cupboard doors. Eye-level ovens prevent children burning themselves on hot doors.

ABOVE: TWO ROOMS HAVE BEEN KNOCKED TOGETHER TO CREATE AN INCLUSIVE MULTIPURPOSE SPACE. THE NEW KITCHEN AND EATING AREA OCCUPY WHAT WAS FORMERLY THE BACK ROOM.

LEFT: A RAISED STEEL UPSTAND FUNCTIONS BOTH AS A SERVING AREA AND A MEANS OF SCREENING KITCHEN ACTIVITY IN A GENERAL LIVING AREA.

continued

# Inclusive kitchens

### Degrees of separation

Any multipurpose or dual-purpose space can descend into chaos without an element of definition. The shape of the room can offer a useful way of making a distinction between different activities: an L-shape, for example, provides a natural break.

A change of flooring material can also signal a shift of activity. The flooring in the kitchen area should be practical and easy to maintain, but you may prefer something more comfortable underfoot in the part of the space devoted to eating and relaxation. Choosing materials that are tonally very similar, such as light ceramic tile with pale wood, is a subtle way of achieving this.

A single wall plane picked out in a vivid colour or papered with a bold print can provide a focus for an eating area.

The inclusive kitchen means that cooking is carried out in public view. For both practical and psychological reasons, it is useful to provide some degree of separation between the kitchen area and the rest of the space. Cooking requires concentration and a barrier of some kind helps to keep distractions at bay and also serves to hide mess. You can arrange the kitchen so that a counter with a raised upstand separates it from the rest of the space or you can screen the working area with sliding doors. Open shelf units also make good spatial dividers.

ABOVE: IN AN INCLUSIVE KITCHEN COOKING IS CARRIED OUT IN PUBLIC VIEW. HERE ONLY THE FURNITURE ARRANGEMENT DEFINES THE SHIFT IN ACTIVITIES.

RIGHT: THE ARM OF AN L-SHAPED SEATING UNIT DIVIDES A KITCHEN AND LIVING AREA WITHOUT CREATING A FORMAL BARRIER.

continued

# Inclusive kitchens

### Practical considerations

- Cooking can be a hot, steamy affair. It is important to provide adequate systems of extraction in any kitchen, and all the more so if the kitchen occupies part of a general living area. You will need a decent ventilation hood to remove greasy vapours and dispel stale cooking odours. It is also a good idea to arrange the kitchen layout so that it benefits from cross-ventilation through opening windows or doors.

- Noise is another consideration. Many people like to include laundry machines in their kitchens, which is all very well if you can leave the room while they are running. Unless you enjoy the background noise of a washing machine or the rumble of a dryer, it is best to install them in another location, such as a utility area or bathroom, and thus maintain a more peaceful atmosphere.

- Wielding sharp knives, handling hot pans and making fine judgements about quantities requires adequate task lighting. Kitchen lighting needs to be targeted directly above the work area. For sociable activities, on the other hand, light levels should be lower and more diffuse. In the inclusive kitchen, it is important to fit the task or directional lights in the kitchen area with a dimmer switch so that you can vary the mood when you sit down at the table.

ABOVE: WHERE POSSIBLE, KITCHENS SHOULD BE SITED NEAR AN OUTSIDE DOOR FOR GOOD VENTILATION.

LEFT: TOP LIGHTING BATHES A KITCHEN IN NATURAL LIGHT. THE PROFESSIONAL-STYLE FLEXIBLE HOSE STANDS OUT AS A SCULPTURAL ELEMENT.

# Small kitchens

Not everyone wants or needs a large kitchen. If you like to eat out regularly or you do not enjoy cooking, it makes sense to devote less space to a kitchen and more to other living spaces.

For many people, however, a small kitchen is not a matter of choice. If this is the case, you can take heart from the fact that many professional chefs actually prefer compact kitchens, where everything they need is right to hand and little time and effort is wasted trotting to and fro. Working in a small, well-planned kitchen is a lot like operating an efficient machine so your cooking need not be limited to simple meals.

**Layout**

Most successful small kitchens are fully fitted. A fitted layout maximizes floor area and also looks neater. It is worth spending considerable time during the planning stage to get things right. Small kitchens must at least be able to accommodate one-person operations devoted more or less exclusively to cooking, and you will need to ensure that the layout supports the way you like to work.

Bear in mind that when you buy fitted units, you are buying space. Make the most of kitchen storage by customizing the interiors of cupboards and drawers with pull-out baskets, racks and adjustable shelving so that you make full use of height, depth and breadth.

ABOVE: FOLD-DOWN OR PULL-OUT ELEMENTS, SUCH AS THIS BREAKFAST COUNTER, ARE GREAT SPACE-SAVING FEATURES FOR THE SMALL KITCHEN.

RIGHT: IN A COMPACT KITCHEN, FITTED UNITS MAKE THE MOST OF THE AVAILABLE STORAGE SPACE, KEEPING WORKTOPS CLEAR FOR FOOD PREPARATION.

continued

# Small kitchens

### Equipping small kitchens

In a small kitchen every single item must earn
its keep. You cannot afford to waste precious
worktop space by cluttering it up with gadgets
that you do not use very often. Many good cooks
can produce elaborate meals with only a
minimum of kitchen equipment. Good quality
knives, pots and pans, and basic utensils are
essential, but specialist equipment such as fish
kettles, pasta-makers and olive-stoners may
well not be.

Take the same approach to cookware and
tableware. Oven-to-tableware avoids the need
for separate serving dishes. Tumblers can be
used for water, juice, beer or wine. Plain
crockery can be used both for everyday and on
special occasions. Keeping it simple means you
will need to store less.

Slim-line or small-scale appliances can also
help to save space in a small kitchen. If you live
alone, small appliances may serve your needs
well and can represent a good investment.

Most small kitchens tend to be short of
worktop space. Pull-out or flap-down panels that
serve as additional preparation areas can be very
useful. Similar features can provide a tabletop or
counter to eat at.

ABOVE: CEILING-HEIGHT CUPBOARDS EXPLOIT THE
STORAGE POTENTIAL IN A TALL, NARROW KITCHEN.

LEFT: OPEN SHELVING AND HANGING RAILS ARE
EFFICIENT STORAGE OPTIONS. AVOID STACKS OF
SPECIALIST EQUIPMENT IN A SMALL KITCHEN AND
FOCUS ON GOOD QUALITY ESSENTIALS.

continued

# Small kitchens

### Enhancing space

A successful small kitchen does not have to feel small. There are a number of decorative and design strategies that you can employ to enhance the sense of space.

- Keep decoration light and simple. Stick to a limited palette of colours and materials to avoid visual busyness. Pale colours and reflective surfaces, such as glass and stainless steel, help to spread around available light.
- Opt for simplicity when you are choosing kitchen cabinetry. Smooth flush doors and drawer fronts create a cleaner and more streamlined appearance than those with textured mouldings.
- Omit the plinth at the base of fitted units to expose the feet. When the floor is uninterrupted, a space looks bigger.
- Consider installing new internal openings in partition walls to overcome any feeling of enclosure. Internal openings also borrow light from adjacent areas, which enhances the sense of space.
- If your kitchen is a self-contained space, consider removing the door so that it does not feel closed in. You can also remove the portion of wall above the door so that the ceiling plane is uninterrupted.
- Recessed or fitted lighting will provide discreet illumination in a tightly planned room. Lights should be carefully positioned so that you are not working in your own shadow.

ABOVE: AN EXCEPTIONALLY COMPACT KITCHEN OCCUPIES A RECESS WITHIN A WALL OF SHELVING. WHEN THE PANELLED DOORS ARE CLOSED, IT BECOMES PART OF THE ARCHITECTURAL FABRIC OF THE ROOM.

RIGHT: HERE, WHITE CABINETS, A GLASS SPLASHBACK AND STAINLESS STEEL WORKTOP REFLECT LIGHT FROM A KITCHEN WINDOW TO CREATE A BRIGHT AIRY SPACE.

# Indoor/outdoor kitchens

Food always seems to taste better outside. Kitchens with an easy connection to an outdoor area allow you to eat and even cook outdoors whenever the weather permits.

## Blurring the boundaries

To create a kitchen that flows seamlessly into an outside space, you can replace single doors or small windows with an expanse of glazing that opens out or slides back.

With open and easy access, a courtyard or garden becomes an outside room for eating and relaxing, as well as a space for children to play in. To enhance the connection between indoors and out, you can extend the same type of flooring (or tone of flooring) from the kitchen to the outside, such as wooden floorboards giving way to decking or stone tiles repeated on both sides of the boundary. A related strategy is to extend a kitchen counter right into the garden, where it can serve as a worktop for outdoor cooking and a storage place for barbecues, garden tools and toys.

Glazed kitchen extensions to the side and the rear are another way of merging indoors with out. Low-E, or low-emissivity, glass prevents excessive heat loss in winter. For kitchens on upper levels, top glazing provides a hint of the world outside, as well as the invigorating quality of natural light.

ABOVE: FRENCH DOORS ALLOW SUNLIGHT TO FLOOD INTO A KITCHEN, BRINGING THE OUTSIDE IN.

LEFT: BIFOLDING GLAZED DOORS OPEN DIRECTLY ONTO A TERRACE, MERGING INDOORS WITH OUT.

continued

# Indoor/outdoor kitchens

### Cooking & eating outside

Part of the pleasure of cooking and eating outside is the easy, uncomplicated nature of the experience: simple food, grilled more often than not, and no standing on ceremony. Impromptu arrangements are fine, such as a picnic on a blanket spread under a shady tree, but for a true indoor/outdoor kitchen, it is worth putting more effort into it.

Set up an outdoor eating area where there is a level surface and some shade – all the better if there is an attractive viewpoint, too. Look for sturdy garden furniture, preferably designs that are foldable or stackable, and which are light enough to be moved indoors during the winter. Garden lighting with candles, flares or lanterns adds a magical dimension to evening meals.

There is a huge range of barbecues and outdoor grills on the market, from disposable trays to expensive all-singing all-dancing rotisseries. A good mid-range option is the drum or lidded bowl barbecue that concentrates heat to allow food to cook evenly all the way through. As an alternative, you can construct your own grill as a permanent outdoor feature.

It is a small step from cooking and eating outside to growing your own fruit and vegetables. No garden is too small for a modest crop of salad vegetables nurtured in grow-bags or container-grown herbs.

ABOVE: FOR SERIOUS DEVOTEES OF OUTDOOR EATING, A PERMANENT PROFESSIONAL-STYLE GRILL OR ROTISSERIE CAN BE A GOOD INVESTMENT.

RIGHT: THE SIMPLICITY OF COOKING OVER AN OPEN FIRE IS PART OF THE PLEASURE OF EATING OUTDOORS. GOOD RESULTS CAN BE ACHIEVED WITH EVEN THE MOST BASIC OF BARBECUE EQUIPMENT.

# Larders

The larder, the traditional adjunct to the kitchen where most food supplies used to be kept, is a time-honoured kitchen feature deserving of revival. In these energy conscious times, the natural refrigeration provided by a larder can help to reduce our dependency on refrigerators for food storage.

A larder is traditionally sited on the side of the house that receives the least sun (north-facing in the northern hemisphere). It should have as many external walls as possible – at least two and ideally three – and should be well ventilated. Usually built with stone floors and slate shelves to maintain coolness, a larder provides an ideal environment for keeping fruit, vegetables, ham, sausages and salamis, game, cheese and preserves. The deep chill of a refrigerator can adversely affect flavour, but a larder keeps food fresh while allowing flavour to mature.

If you do not have the opportunity to construct a larder or do not have a suitable space that could be converted into one, a pantry cupboard might make a good alternative (although without the natural cooling). Pantry cupboards, generally supplied by specialist kitchen companies, are tall, freestanding or built-in units, often with double doors. They can be customized inside with earthenware bread crocks, vegetable baskets, shelves and wine racks.

ABOVE: A WALK-IN LARDER TRADITIONALLY HAS A STONE OR TILED FLOOR WHICH HELPS TO KEEP IT COOL.

LEFT: IN A PANTRY CUPBOARD, FRESH FOOD AND PROVISIONS CAN BE STORED CONVENIENTLY IN ONE PLACE FOR EASY ACCESS.

# INTRODUCTION
# PLANNING & LAYOUT
# FIXTURES & FITTINGS
# DECOR & DETAIL

# Basic considerations

Rapid changes in technology have dramatically increased the range of functions performed by kitchen appliances and most are to some degree 'smart' these days. At the same time, white goods are no longer exclusively white, but come in a range of colours, finishes and styles, from the cutting edge to self-consciously retro. Taken together, these factors mean that deciding which kitchen appliances to buy is no longer a question of simple choices.

- When technology makes life simpler it is well worth the investment. Decide which functions you will actually use before you invest in a machine that is more sophisticated (and expensive) than you require.
- Saving energy is another key consideration. Invest for the long term (and the planet) and opt for appliances with the highest energy effiency ratings.
- Think about maintenance. Certain finishes, such as stainless steel, require more upkeep. You do not want to spend more time cleaning than you do cooking and preparing food.
- Style is seductive. While it is good to have the option to buy a siren-red refrigerator these days, basic practicality should never be sacrificed for good looks.
- Research the market carefully before making a major purchase. Independent consumer magazines and websites provide comprehensive and objective information about the performance, durability and value for money of different brands and models.

ABOVE: PIERCED STEEL BOXES MAKE ROBUST CONTAINERS FOR BASIC KIT. DECIDE WHICH GADGETS AND EQUIPMENT YOU REALLY NEED AND ARE LIKELY TO MAKE FULL USE OF.

RIGHT: AN IMPRESSIVE DOUBLE-RANGE COOKER IS IDEAL FOR PRODUCING FOOD ON A LARGE SCALE BUT TAKES UP A SUBSTANTIAL AMOUNT OF SPACE.

# Lighting

The kitchen is the hardest working area in the home and requires up to two or three times as much light as areas devoted to relaxation. Without good illumination, kitchen activities such as using sharp knives and handling hot pans can become hazardous. At the same time, kitchens are increasingly social areas, so it is a good idea to build in some flexibility to a lighting scheme. Unless a kitchen is used exclusively for cooking, a combination of bright task lighting, correctly angled and positioned over worktops and appliances, and warm ambient or background lighting is preferable.

**Types of light source**
- Energy wasting incandescent (tungsten) light bulbs are being gradually phased out and many of the brighter wattages are no longer available. Instead, you can opt for energy efficient compact fluorescents. These come in a wide range of shapes and can be fitted into every conceivable kind of light fixture. Although they are more expensive than tungsten bulbs, fluorescents consume only a fifth of the energy and last 15 times longer.
- Another alternative is low-energy halogen lights, which provide fresh, clean light.
- LEDs, or light emitting diodes, offer a whole spectrum of colours and are being used increasingly in domestic fittings.

ABOVE: DAYLIGHT IS THE MOST ENERGY EFFICIENT LIGHT SOURCE OF ALL. HERE, A KITCHEN IS BATHED IN NATURAL LIGHT FROM A FULLY GLAZED ROOF.

LEFT: A WORKTOP AND GLASS SPLASHBACK ARE EVOCATIVELY LIT BY CONCEALED LIGHTING.

continued

# Lighting

### Designing a lighting scheme

- Fixed forms of lighting, such as downlights, tracklights and spots, make good sense in a kitchen where many elements are fitted.
- Avoid relying on central pendants or ceiling lights as a source of background illumination. These cast shadows into the corners of the room and create a deadening atmosphere. Wall-mounted uplights are better, as are strip lights concealed at the top of wall units.
- Keep freestanding lights and table lamps well away from the kitchen area. Trailing flexes pose a serious hazard.
- Position directional lights so that you are not working in your own shadow. Strip lights mounted on the underside of units are an effective way of lighting a worktop.
- Recessed fittings are neat and unobtrusive. Make sure that light fittings are easy to clean and access.
- Small information lights are useful for deep larder cupboards.
- Reflective surfaces and finishes, such as glass and stainless steel, enhance the level of light. At the same time, ensure that you do not create glare, which can be just as dangerous as low light.
- If you eat in the kitchen, put the task lighting on a dimmer switch, so that you can lower light levels when you are sitting at the table.

ABOVE: WHITE CABINETS, WORKTOP AND WALLS DISTRIBUTE LIGHT FROM A STRIP LIGHT CONCEALED BEHIND A WALL-MOUNTED BAFFLE.

RIGHT: INTERNAL LIGHTING GLOWS SOFTLY THROUGH THE FROSTED GLASS PANELS OF THESE CABINETS.

# Worktops & splashbacks

Worktops take a great deal of punishment and need to be able to resist heat and stains as well as knocks. Whichever material you choose will depend on your budget and the overall style of your kitchen. Bear in mind that a good quality worktop, in stone, for example, can lift a simple fitted kitchen out of the ordinary.

### Practical considerations

- Thick worktops are the most durable. Opt for the thickest worktop you can afford. The most common thicknesses are 30mm (1¼in) and 40mm (1½in). A 40mm worktop will have greater resistance to heat and be less prone to cracking or warping.
- If possible, the worktop should be fitted as a single length. Otherwise, keep joins to a minimum so that bacteria cannot build up in the crevices. Similarly, sinks should be fitted flush with the top or under-mounted.
- Splashbacks, which protect the portion of the wall between the worktop and the upper cupboards (if any), must first and foremost be water-resistant and easy to clean. The area behind the hob must also be resistant to heat. A single continuous surface is visually neat. Even better is to opt for a combined worktop and splashback that is totally seam-free.

LEFT: 'METRO-STYLE' TILES MAKE A PRACTICAL AND GOOD-LOOKING SPLASHBACK WHICH COMPLIMENTS THE RETRO SINK AND HARDWOOD WORKTOP.

RIGHT: IN AN ULTRA-MODERN KITCHEN A SEAMLESS GLASS SPLASHBACK IS EASY TO MAINTAIN.

continued

# Worktops & splashbacks

### Materials

- **Wood** Inherently hygienic, wood must be treated to withstand heat and moisture, and finishes need to be re-applied regularly. Oiled hardwood is the best option, but can be expensive; end-grain glued together in blocks or strips makes a strong, dense surface; and lacquered softwood is a cheaper alternative. If using oak, make sure to seal it properly, as without doing so, the base of damp cast iron pans and casseroles can stain the oak black leaving it almost impossible to remove.

- **Stone** With a natural beauty, stone is available in a huge range of colours, textures and finishes. Marble and limestone make attractive worktops, but stain easily and must be adequately sealed. Polished granite is an equally attractive option and is heatproof, waterproof and stain-resistant. Units may need bracing to support the weight.

- **Composites** Manufactured from resins and minerals, composites are highly durable, can be cut or moulded into any shape required and come in a vast range of colours.

- **Glass** This is a good option for splashbacks. It is easy to wipe clean and is attractive when backlit or coloured.

- **Laminates** These are synthetic products made of layers of paper and resins fused and glued to a wooden substrate. They are reasonably priced, come in a wide range of colours and patterns, and are easy to maintain. They cannot be repaired once damaged.

- **Concrete** With a rugged, industrial appearance, concrete can be cast *in situ* or designed to individual specification.

- **Stainless steel** Available in various finishes, from shiny to matt, stainless steel looks professional and is relatively expensive, but tends to show up fingerprints and smudges.

ABOVE: COMPOSITE, CONCRETE OR STONE WORKTOPS CAN BE CUSTOM MADE WITH INTEGRAL SINKS.

RIGHT: A BESPOKE MARBLE WORKTOP RUNS THE LENGTH OF A KITCHEN AND EATING AREA. MARBLE MUST BE SEALED TO PREVENT STAINING.

# Sinks

### Sink formats

When choosing a sink, you must first decide whether you need one, two or three bowls. One large sink is usually enough if you already have a dishwasher; one-and-a-half is a more practical option for washing up by hand.

- Rectangular sinks make better use of space than round ones.
- Inset sinks are the most common type of sink. The lip sits on top of the worktop and the edge is sealed to make it waterproof.
- Flush-mounted and under-mounted sinks are neater and more hygienic options than inset sinks.
- Integral sinks made of the same material as the worktop, such as stainless steel or a composite such as Corian, are neat, hygienic and hardwearing.
- Freestanding sink units are also available. These modular workstations have a contemporary professional look.

### Materials

- **Stainless steel** The most common material for sinks, stainless steel is tough, heat-resistant and hygienic. Thicker gauge steel is quieter and sturdier than thinner, cheaper types. Brushed or satin finishes are less likely to show scratches than polished ones.
- **Ceramic** A ceramic sink looks at home in either a traditional or contemporary kitchen. Oblong Belfast sinks have a country-style appeal. Cast-iron sinks coated with porcelain enamel are widely available in every colour.

- **Composite** Sinks made of composite materials such as Corian are warm, durable and highly resistant to damage. They can be detailed as part of a single continuous surface comprising worktop, sink and splashback.
- **Vitreous enamelled steel** A smooth, hard surface often available in different colours. Be aware that a vitreous enamelled surface can be easily damaged by heavy cast iron pots and pans.

ABOVE: A CONTEMPORARY DOUBLE-BOWL CERAMIC SINK HAS A LIPPED EDGE THAT SITS ON TOP OF THE WORKTOP. SOME MODERN SINKS INCORPORATE SLIDING DRAINERS OR CHOPPING BOARDS.

LEFT: PERIOD OR TRADITIONAL-STYLE SINKS COME IN CERAMIC OR CAST-IRON COVERED WITH PORCELAIN ENAMEL. SALVAGE YARDS CAN BE GOOD SOURCES OF RECLAIMED FITTINGS.

# Taps

Taps are in frequent use and must work properly and operate easily. You need to be able to rotate the tap freely so that you can direct water into different parts of the sink or sinks. Ceramic disc technology allows modern taps to be drip free – taps that rely on washers to control water flow often tend to leak. Good-quality taps are sculptural objects in their own right and can represent a relatively affordable way of adding a touch of class to a simple kitchen. The finishes that are available for taps include stainless steel, chrome, brass, epoxy of different colours, pewter and nickel.

- Mixer taps combine hot and cold water in the same flow. Many contemporary versions have single-lever controls.
- Pillar taps keep water temperatures separate. Bridge mixers have separate hot and cold taps joined to a central spout. Both are traditional in appearance.
- Wall-mounted or high-rise taps are a good choice if you have a deep or wide sink or if you need to fill tall pans or buckets.
- Professional-style taps feature a long flexible hose for rinsing pans and dishes and washing areas around the sink. Alternatively, some taps include a pull-out spray head.
- Water-filtering mixer taps provide hot, cold and filtered water.
- Quarter-turn taps can be turned fully on or off with just a 90-degree movement.

LEFT: THIS KITCHEN TAP FEATURES A PULL-OUT SPRAY HEAD WHICH MAKES IT EASY TO CLEAN THE SINK THOROUGHLY AND FILL DEEP POTS AND PANS.

RIGHT: LIKE MANY CONEMPORARY DESIGNS, THIS SIMPLE, UNFUSSY TAP HAS A SINGLE-LEVER CONTROL.

# Cookers, ovens & hobs

The cooker is the key kitchen appliance. Before you make an investment, research the market thoroughly and attend demonstrations if necessary to make sure you are buying a product that meets your needs. Think about the way you cook and what you like to cook.

- A single appliance that combines hot rings or burners with an oven and grill is easy to install and slot into place. A separate hob and oven may require a kitchen overhaul.
- If you have the choice, do you prefer cooking with gas or electricity? A gas hob and an electric oven is a popular combination.
- Make sure you choose the right size and capacity. Does the hob have enough burners? Is the oven big enough (think of the size of a Christmas turkey)?
- The two main types of extractors are ducted extractor fans, which remove greasy vapours completely and need to be positioned on or near an exterior wall, and recirculating fans, which purify the air.
- For energy-efficiency, look for products with the highest rating.

## Cookers

- Single stand-alone cookers can be either electric or gas and come in a range of prices.
- Agas and other cast-iron ranges are heavy and must be installed on a solid level floor.
- For the serious cook, range cookers offer an enviable array of functions: multiple burners, including special features such as wok burners and griddle plates, double ovens, separate grills and warm storage drawers.

ABOVE: HOBS MAY BE ELECTRIC, GAS OR INDUCTION, OR A COMBINATION OF ALL THREE. SOME INCLUDE SPECIAL FEATURES SUCH AS WOK BURNERS.

LEFT: THE AGA, WHICH MAY BE FUELLED IN DIFFERENT WAYS, COMBINES MANY FUNCTIONS IN ONE APPLIANCE, FROM BAKING AND ROASTING, TO TOASTING, STIR-FRYING AND STEAMING.

continued

# Cookers, ovens & hobs

## Ovens

- Conventional electric ovens radiate heat from top and bottom, which means that the centre is the best place to cook food.
- Fan-assisted electric ovens require very little pre-heating and cook food evenly wherever it is placed.
- Multifunction electric ovens can be used with or without fan assistance and many provide up to ten different settings for cooking particular types of food.
- In gas ovens it is easier to regulate the heat and food stays moister for longer. Fan-assisted gas ovens are energy saving and provide even temperatures inside the oven.
- Pyrolytic self-cleaning ovens heat up to 500°C (932°F) and burn off grease and food deposits.

## Hobs

- Gas hobs are popular because they provide instant controllable heat. Most are four-burner, but five-burners are more versatile. Some models include a wok burner and even a fish-kettle burner.
- Electric hobs come in many different forms: sealed plate hobs are easy to clean but slow to heat up and cool down; ceramic glass hobs are smooth and streamlined; induction hobs transfer heat directly to the bottom of the pan, but only certain pans work with them.
- Domino hobs are modular two-plate hobs that can be assembled in any configuration: gas, ceramic, grill or wok.

ABOVE: AN EXTRACTOR POSITIONED ABOVE THE HOB IS ESSENTIAL FOR REMOVING GREASY AIR AND ODOURS. MANY ALSO INCORPORATE TASK LIGHTING.

RIGHT: ALL-IN-ONE COOKERS COMBINE A HOB WITH AN OVEN AND GRILL. THIS RETRO VERSION INCLUDES AN OVERHEAD RACK FOR PLATE-WARMING.

# Refrigerators & freezers

It is important to choose a refrigerator or freezer based on your way of life, the size of your family and the way you cook and shop. There is a vast range of appliances on the market, from small basic models that fit underneath a worktop to huge double-door refrigerators that have many special features and functions.

- Decide whether you want a refrigerator with an ice box or a separate refrigerator and freezer. Larder refrigerators, which do not have freezer compartments, offer more space for fresh food. Freezer compartments have star ratings, which show how long certain kinds of frozen foods can be kept.
- Do you want a freestanding appliance or one that is built-in? Integrated refrigerators are designed to be covered with a front panel that matches the rest of your units. Many freestanding refrigerators make bold style statements in their own right.
- Choose a refrigerator that is big enough for your needs and will fit into the space at your disposal. If you are installing a standard refrigerator under a worktop, you should allow a gap of 25mm (1in) at the top, back and sides for ventilation.
- Modern appliances are highly energy-efficient, which makes them relatively cheap to run. Many models are also free of CFCs and HFCs, which contribute to global warming.

LEFT: STAND-ALONE RETRO-STYLE REFRIGERATORS HAVE BECOME VERY POPULAR IN RECENT YEARS AND ARE AVAILABLE IN A RANGE OF COLOURS.

ABOVE: A STAINLESS STEEL REFRIGERATOR IS NEATLY INTEGRATED INTO A FITTED KITCHEN TO FORM ONE OF THE POINTS OF THE 'WORK TRIANGLE'.

continued

# Refrigerators & freezers

### Features & functions

- Auto defrost regulates the temperature inside the refrigerator to prevent the build up of frost. Larder refrigerators have auto defrost. Refrigerators with integral iceboxes need to be defrosted when ice builds up or they will not chill food adequately.
- Intelligent cooling, where the temperature is controlled electronically and displayed on an LCD panel, maintains an even temperature throughout the refrigerator. If the door is left open for a while, cool air will be directed temporarily to warmer areas.
- A 'quick chill' function allows you to chill fresh food quickly.
- Some refrigerators have antibacterial coating on the walls and door to promote hygiene.
- Shelves and internal fittings vary. Glass shelves are better than wire ones because they stay cool and are easier to clean. Adjustable shelving, bottle and egg racks and compartments for butter and cheese are standard, as are salad drawers or crispers.
- Some refrigerators feature multi-zone cooling, which allows different foods to be cooled to the right temperature. These may include special meat drawers, humidity controlled salad drawers, and a zero degree chiller compartment for ready meals.
- Some large refrigerators include an ice and chilled water dispenser on the freezer side. These appliances need to be plumbed within 1m (3ft) of a water supply.

ABOVE: A COMBINED REFRIGERATOR AND FREEZER IS MORE VERSATILE THAN A REFRIGERATOR WITH AN INTERIOR ICEBOX. SOME REFRIGERATORS INCORPORATE A CHILLER COMPARTMENT FOR READY MEALS.

RIGHT: IF YOU HAVE A BIG FAMILY, A LARGE REFRIGERATOR SUCH AS THIS ONE WILL PROVIDE EFFICIENT MULTIPURPOSE FOOD STORAGE.

# Dishwashers

Dishwashers are not indispensable, unlike other kitchen appliances, but they do save time and effort. Top-range models use much less water and energy than washing the equivalent load of dishes by hand and the results are usually better.

- When choosing a dishwasher, first assess your needs and how much space you have. Full-size dishwashers have the capacity to wash 12 place settings (excluding pans and serving dishes). Slimline models take nine place settings and compact versions take four.
- Most dishwashers are designed to fit under a worktop. Some are integrated appliances, which can be concealed behind a panel to match your units. Site the dishwasher as close as possible to the sink to make plumbing more straightforward.
- Programmes vary according to the machine and may include an 'eco' setting, a setting for glassware, a half-load setting and a rinse programme. 'Intelligent' dishwashers can assess how dirty a load is and adjust the programme accordingly.
- The most efficient machines have two revolving spray arms fitted top and bottom.
- Look out for flexible interior fittings that accommodate different sizes of dishes and types of utensil.
- An anti-flood sensor, which cuts off the water supply in the case of a leak, is a useful feature.
- Stainless steel interiors are more robust than enamel but can cause some metals to discolour. Use a flat cutlery basket in the top of the machine to wash silver cutlery.

ABOVE: DISHWASHERS SHOULD BE SITED AS CLOSE TO THE KITCHEN SINK AS POSSIBLE TO MAKE PLUMBING MORE STRAIGHTFORWARD.

LEFT: INTEGRAL DISHWASHERS ARE DESIGNED TO BE CONCEALED BEHIND A FRONT PANEL THAT MATCHES THE REST OF YOUR KITCHEN UNITS.

# Laundry

Many people like to include laundry appliances in the kitchen. If you have the option, however, it is perhaps more practical to site washing machines and tumble dryers elsewhere in the home in order to avoid sacrificing valuable kitchen storage space. Noise levels from laundry appliances, which might compromise the kitchen's function as a social area, are something else to bear in mind. From an ecological perspective, you might think about managing without an energy hungry tumble dryer altogether and line-drying your clothes instead.

## Washing machines

- The types of washing machine available are top loaders, front loaders and integrated appliances that form part of a fitted kitchen.
- The variety of programmes and settings can be confusing, so think carefully about your requirements and do not buy a machine that is more complicated than you need. A Hand Wash programme, for example, would be useful if you have a lot of delicate clothes.
- Choose a machine with a high energy efficiency rating and which uses less water.
- Washing machines with fast spins produce drier clothes and reduce the amount of time you need to use a tumble dryer.

## Dryers

- Vented dryers expel hot air to the outside via a hose and must be sited on an external wall.
- Condenser dryers convert hot air to water, which is collected in a reservoir. They are noisier, more expensive and slower.

## Washer-dryers

- A washer-dryer is a useful solution if space is short, but will perform less well than a single-function machine.
- Normally only half of a washload can be dried at one time.

LEFT: TOP-LOADING LAUNDRY APPLIANCES REDUCE THE STRAIN ON YOUR BACK AND CAN BE SAFER IF THERE ARE YOUNG CHILDREN IN THE HOUSEHOLD.

RIGHT: A PULL-OUT AND LIFT-UP IRONING BOARD, WHICH IS STORED IN A DRAWER, MAKES A NEAT SPACE-SAVING FEATURE FOR A SMALL KITCHEN.

# Small appliances & basic kit

You do not have to be a master chef to find specialist cooking tools and utensils appealing. The important question to ask yourself before you succumb to a purchase is how often you will use a particular appliance or piece of kit.

**Small appliances**

Aside from kettles and toasters, few small appliances are indispensable. Which ones you choose will depend on the way you cook.

- Microwaves, commonly used for reheating and defrosting food and for cooking ready meals, use electromagnetic waves to heat food. Programmes vary: some allow you to steam and combination microwaves allow you to roast or grill food in half the time it would take in a conventional oven. Power, performance and size vary. Models are either freestanding or designed to be built into base or wall units.

- Food processors speed up food preparation and can be used to make anything from soup to pastry. They do not always make simple chopping and slicing tasks quicker, however, once you take into account the amount of time it takes to assemble them and clean the parts when you have finished.

- Appliances such as bread-makers, pasta-makers, coffee machines and electric juicers are the types of specialist item that it is only worth giving house room to if you use them on a weekly or daily basis.

ABOVE: A BASIC SET OF GOOD QUALITY POTS AND PANS IS EASY TO STORE AND SHOULD SERVE MOST OF YOUR COOKING REQUIREMENTS.

LEFT: WHATEVER YOU KEEP ON THE COUNTER SHOULD BE IN FREQUENT USE. ENSURE THAT YOU HAVE ENOUGH POWER POINTS TO AVOID OVERLOADING SOCKETS.

continued

# Small appliances & basic kit

## Basic kit

Quality, not quantity, is what makes a kitchen well-equipped. Spending money on high-grade equipment will always be worth the investment.

- Good knives are fundamental. Invest in the best you can afford and keep them in good condition. Store them in a block, rack or magnetic holder so they do not blunt too quickly. You will need at least three knives in different sizes, as well as a carving knife and a bread knife with a serrated edge. Carbon steel knives last the longest, but need to be well cared for to prevent rusting. Stainless steel does not corrode in the same way, but can be harder to sharpen.
- Good quality pots and pans will also repay investment. Stainless steel pans with heavy bases are easy to clean and spread heat evenly. Copper pans, while expensive, conduct heat even more efficiently and serious cooks swear by them. Cast-iron casseroles are ideal for stews and slow cooking. You will also need a roasting tin and frying pan, and a wok if you like to stir-fry.
- Basic utensils include whisks, graters, chopping boards, peelers, lemon squeezers, sieves, colanders, can openers, corkscrews, wooden spoons, ladles, kitchen scissors, slotted spoons, spatulas, measuring jugs, weighing scales and mixing bowls. Try not to clutter up your drawers and cupboards with specialist utensils such as melon-ballers or hard-boiled egg slicers that you will not use very often.

ABOVE: A NARROW SLOT FITTED WITH RODS STORES KITCHEN TOWELS AND TRAYS NEXT TO THE HOB.

RIGHT: CLASSIC BONE-HANDLED CUTLERY WILL LAST A LIFETIME, BUT IT NEEDS TO BE WASHED BY HAND. PUTTING IT IN THE DISHWASHER WILL SHRINK AND DISCOLOUR THE HANDLES.

# Storage

Kitchens house a diverse range of things from fresh food to washing powder, cornflakes to bin bags, crockery to can openers. Well-organized storage is vital to keep essentials in optimum condition and within easy reach.

- Organize your kitchen so that what you use frequently is kept near the relevant area of activity. For example, pots and pans should be stored near the cooker or hob in a cupboard, deep pull-out pan drawer or suspended by hooks. Frequently used kitchen utensils can be kept in a jar or hanging from a rack.
- Store spices and basic condiments near the food preparation area, but bear in mind that spices and herbs lose their flavour if they are kept for too long or too close to a source of heat.
- Decant open packages of dried food into sealed storage jars to maintain freshness and prevent spoiling by insects or mice.
- Do not store heavy or bulky items too high up or too low down. Easy reach is somewhere between eye level and knee level.
- Anything that is used less than once a fortnight, such as large serving platters, can be stored away from the main centres of activity or perhaps out of the kitchen altogether.

ABOVE: AN 'APPLIANCE GARAGE' FOR STORING SMALL KITCHEN APPLIANCES HAS A SLIDING TAMBOUR FRONT.

LEFT: A DEEP DRAWER IS FITTED WITH AN INTERIOR RACK TO STORE DISHES. A 'SOFT-CLOSE' MECHANISM WILL PREVENT THE DRAWER FROM JARRING.

continued

# Storage

### Fitted units

- Whatever style of fitted unit you choose, look out for carcases that are 18mm (7in) thick and made of MDF, which is stable and warps less than solid wood. Adjustable legs take account of any unevenness in the floor.
- Drawers should have solid sides, strong bases and run smoothly. It is more practical to include a block of drawers within a run of fitted units, rather than having a single drawer at the top of each unit.
- Special units, such as corner units, allow you to make the most of available space.

- Customize the interior of fitted units with adjustable shelves, dividers, baskets, wire trays and other accessories. Shelves of varying depth and height allow you to group similar packages or items in the same location, so that nothing gets pushed to the back and forgotten about it.
- Make use of the back of cupboard doors to store pan lids or other flat items.
- 'Easy-on' hinges that allow doors to open and remain plumb with the frame are neat and easy to use. Sliding doors are a good idea if space is tight.

ABOVE: SEMI-TRANSPARENT PANELS MINIMIZE THE IMPACT OF WALL-HUNG CUPBOARDS AND ALLOW YOU TO READ THEIR CONTENTS AT A GLANCE.

RIGHT: TALL AND NARROW PANTRY CUPBOARDS ARE GOOD FOR STORING BASIC PROVISIONS. THEY SHOULD PULL OUT EASILY ON WELL-FITTED RUNNERS.

continued

# Storage

### Storage furniture

Freestanding pieces of storage furniture, such as dressers or retro-style 'maid-savers', make good places to keep cutlery, crockery and glassware. If your kitchen includes an eating area, position the dresser midway between the dining table and the kitchen proper, so that it is easy to unload the dishwasher and set the table.

- Drawer dividers are essential for keeping cutlery tidy. It is important to keep silver flatware separate from stainless steel, preferably in a felt-lined canteen.
- Glasses should never be stored upside down on their rims.
- Do not hang delicate cups up by their handles, which is the weakest part.
- Stack plates and bowls in short piles of six to eight. Group sizes and patterns together.

### Out on view

Whatever you keep out on view – on open shelves or suspended from racks and rails – should be in constant use. Anything superfluous to requirements simply occupies valuable space and attracts dust and grease.

### Waste management

Allocate a dedicated area for separate recycling bins to allow you to manage kitchen waste efficiently. Neat colour-coded or labelled bins make it easy to sort paper, plastic, metal and glass packaging. For optimum efficiency recycle organic waste in a compost heap or wormery.

ABOVE: THIS CONTEMPORARY DRESSER HAS ALL THE TRADITIONAL FEATURES, AS WELL AS A RACK FOR STORING WINE AND WICKER BINS FOR VEGETABLES.

LEFT: THE APPEARANCE OF A KITCHEN IS LARGELY DEFINED BY THE WAY YOU APPROACH STORAGE, HOW MUCH IS CONCEALED AND HOW MUCH IS LEFT ON VIEW.

# INTRODUCTION
# PLANNING & LAYOUT
# FIXTURES & FITTINGS
# DECOR & DETAIL

# Basic considerations

While kitchens are intensely practical places, it does not mean style has to take a back seat. Colour, pattern and texture, the fundamental elements of the decorative palette, have just as important a role to play here as they do elsewhere in the home. Their potential to create a distinctive look can be explored in all sorts of ways, from the choice of wall treatment to the finish of kitchen units and appliances.

- Assembling a decorative palette for the kitchen is about choosing materials, first and foremost, and deciding how they will work together. Performance matters and it is important to select the right materials for the job. Surfaces and finishes must be able to withstand kitchen activity and resist stains, oil, heat and water.

- Consider function as well as form when selecting the working details of your kitchen. Good-quality handles, catches, hinges and switches can make all the difference between a kitchen that is simply adequate and one that performs seamlessly and efficiently.

- Expressing your tastes and preferences – particularly what you like to cook and eat – helps to bring your kitchen to life.

ABOVE: WHITE, WITH ITS ASSOCIATION OF CLEANLINESS AND FRESHNESS, REMAINS A POPULAR CHOICE FOR KITCHEN SURFACES AND FINISHES.

RIGHT: SIMPLE STONE FLOORING IS RUGGED AND HARDWEARING. HERE IT EXTENDS FROM THE KITCHEN TO THE OUTDOOR AREA, BLURRING THE BOUNDARIES BETWEEN THE TWO.

## Colour

Colour and the kitchen have not always gone hand in hand. For many years white – clean, fresh and hygienic – reigned supreme, a token of good housekeeping. The popularity of the country kitchen saw natural and neutral shades of cream, brown, terracotta and buff come to the fore, either painted on walls or expressed in materials such as wood, stone and tile.

Nowadays bright, vibrant colour is no stranger to the kitchen. Kitchens have always featured incidental accents of colour – displays of fruit and vegetables, cheerful crockery and pots and pans – but increasingly colour is being used as a way of enhancing space and the quality of natural light and of signalling shifts between one area of activity and another. A wall picked out in strong colour, a vivid run of kitchen units or a luminous splashback can inject a note of optimism and confidence.

- Choose colours based on the quality of natural light. Bright, airy backgrounds make spaces seem bigger. Warm colours provide a sense of enclosure.
- Do not be tempted to overdo it. A single strong shade is enough for most kitchens. Offset this with white or neutral tones.
- Remember that it is cheaper and easier to repaint a wall if you get tired of a colour than it is to replace unit doors or a refrigerator.

ABOVE: GLOSSY BLUE FITTED UNITS MAKE AN EFFECTIVE CONTRAST TO THE NEUTRAL TONES OF THE WHITE TILEWORK AND STRIPPED WOOD FLOOR.

LEFT: SMALL DOSES OF STRONG COLOUR BRING A SENSE OF VITALITY TO A KITCHEN. HERE, A VIBRANT SPLASHBACK INTRODUCES A STRONG RED ACCENT.

# Pattern & texture

## Pattern

Inherently rhythmic and repetitive, pattern brings a sense of movement to an interior. While it is most often and most overtly expressed in soft furnishings and wallpaper designs, which tend to be less practical in a kitchen, it can also be found more subtly in arrangement – a row of spice jars, a display of fresh food or patterned crockery – or as an intrinsic aspect of a particular material – the flecked surface of granite, the grain of wood or a gridded tile floor.

## Texture

Closely allied with pattern is texture. Where colours are subdued and pattern is incidental, textural variety becomes an important way of providing a sense of depth and character. Kitchens are hands-on places. If every surface is uniformly smooth, the result can be a little bland and soulless. Ringing the changes with different materials used on the counter, floor and walls enhances this natural tactility.

While synthetics can be sleek and efficient, natural materials such as wood, stone and ceramic tile provide greater textural interest, not least because they have the potential to age well and even improve with use and maintenance. The same cannot be said of laminate or other plastics.

ABOVE: THE INHERENT BUSYNESS OF PATTERNED TILES IS SUBDUED BY THE BLUE AND WHITE COLOURWAY, RESULTING IN AN ALMOST TEXTURAL EFFECT.

RIGHT: HERE, THE GRAIN EVIDENT IN WOOD FLOORING AND THE GRIDDED APPEARANCE OF TIMBER CLADDING INTRODUCE A DIFFERENT TYPE OF PATTERN WHICH IS CLOSELY ALLIED WITH TEXTURE.

# Wall treatments

The wall treatment you choose can set the tone for your entire kitchen: terracotta tiles or wood panelling create a rustic feel, fresh paint or contemporary wallpaper look more modern.

**Materials**

- **Paint** The easiest way of introducing colour, paint is the cheapest cover-up for kitchen walls and ceilings. Choose a durable finish, such as oil-based eggshell or silk emulsion, which can be wiped down. Some stores sell moisture-resistant paint specifically designed for use in kitchens.
- **Wallpaper** Patterned wallpaper can be used to create a feature wall, anchoring an eating area within a multipurpose space. Choose paper with a washable vinyl coating.
- **Bare plaster and brick** Both of these have a homely quality. Plaster needs to be sealed with matt varnish to protect it from staining.
- **Wood cladding** Tongue-and-groove wood panelling creates a country feel in the kitchen. Wood must be either sealed to protect it against damp and stains or painted. Extra fire protection is required if wood cladding is used near cookers or hobs.
- **Tiles** These are ideal for kitchen walls, particularly next to preparation and cooking areas. Hardwearing, water-resistant and heat-proof, ceramic tiles come in a wide range of formats, sizes, colours and patterns. Tiling looks better if it is whole-hearted.

ABOVE: WOODEN WALLS HAVE A COUNTRIFIED APPEAL. SOFTWOOD MUST BE THOROUGHLY SEALED OR PAINTED TO PREVENT DAMAGE BY WATER PENETRATION.

LEFT: PAINTED BRICK WALLS PROVIDE A TEXTURAL BACKDROP. CHOOSE MOISTURE-RESISTANT PAINT DESIGNED FOR KITCHEN USE.

# Flooring

As with all other kitchen surfaces, flooring should be chosen first and foremost on the basis of practicality.

### Practical considerations

- Standing for long periods on hard floors such as stone can be tiring. Floors with more 'give', such as those made of wood, are much more comfortable underfoot.
- Very smooth or glossy floors are slippery and increase the risk of accidents.
- How easy is the floor to keep clean? Does the floor need to be sealed before use? How often do seals need to be renewed?
- Consider the durability of the material. How long can you expect the floor to last given reasonable maintenance?
- Hard floors can amplify noise uncomfortably in an open-plan space.
- Massive materials such as stone and tile warm up slowly and lose heat slowly, which can be an asset in homes designed with passive solar strategies in mind.
- Some types of flooring, including linoleum, have inherent anti-bacterial properties and are hypo-allergenic, which can be an advantage in households with young children.
- Most types of floor require professional installation. In some cases, this must be done before cabinetry is installed because the floor level will be raised. All flooring must be laid over a dry, even subfloor. Heavy materials, such as stone, should be laid over concrete or a strengthened wooden floor.

ABOVE: STRONG COLOUR IS LESS DOMINANT UNDERFOOT THAN IT IS ON WALLS. RUBBER, LINOLEUM, VINYL AND CERAMIC TILES ARE ALL AVAILABLE IN VIBRANT CONTEMPORARY SHADES.

RIGHT: HERE, A SHIFT IN FLOORING FROM BLACK-AND-WHITE TILING TO HARDWOOD DEFINES DIFFERENT AREAS OF ACTIVITY IN AN OPEN-PLAN SPACE.

continued

# Flooring

## Materials

- **Wood** There is a huge range of species and formats of wood to choose from: hardwood is the most expensive, softwood less so; thick veneered boards are cheaper than solid timber; the least costly is wood laminate. New timber flooring needs to be acclimatized for 48 hours prior to installation.

- **Natural stone** Limestone, slate, granite, sandstone, marble and travertine are all suitable flooring materials. Choose a matt, honed or riven finish to reduce slipperiness. All stone must be sealed to prevent staining.

- **Tiles** Types of tile include porcelain, ceramic and terracotta. Colour, pattern, size and format vary widely. Unglazed tiles need to be sealed to prevent staining.

- **Linoleum** A high-quality natural product, linoleum is available in sheet or tile form, and in many colours and patterns. It is durable, warm, quiet, anti-bacterial and resistant to acids, oils and grease.

- **Vinyl** This is a synthetic flooring available in a vast range of colours, patterns and textures, and comes in both sheet and tile. High-quality vinyl flooring can be expensive, but most types are in the mid- to low-price range. Vinyl flooring is thin, so will not raise the floor level.

- **Cork** A natural flooring, cork is generally available as tiles. It has a limited colour range and must be sealed properly, but is warm, comfortable and quiet.

- **Rubber** There are both synthetic and natural types or rubber and it is available in a huge range of vibrant colours, textures and patterns. It will take any amount of punishment.

ABOVE: SOFTWOOD CAN BE SANDED, SEALED AND PAINTED. HERE, FLOORBOARDS HAVE BEEN PAINTED WHITE TO CREATE A LIGHT AIRY KITCHEN.

LEFT: TEXTURED STONE FLAGS PROVIDE A GOOD NON-SLIP SURFACE. STONE CAN BE CHILLY BUT IT ACQUIRES GREAT DEPTH OF CHARACTER OVER TIME.

# Detail

If decoration largely concerns itself with the big picture, detail is where it all comes into focus. The smaller the kitchen, the closer the focus, and the more important it is to get detailing right, both aesthetically and practically.

- Pay attention to the joins or seams where one surface or material meets another, as well as the joins between sections of the same material, such as a worktop. Tight seams reduce the risk of bacteria building up in crevices. They also create a more unified look. Neat joins between different types of flooring prevents materials from lifting and chipping.
- Make sure that the working parts of cabinetry, such as drawer runners, catches, and other pull-out elements, all operate as smoothly as possible. Any deficiencies in basic practicality will be a source of daily frustration.
- Upgrading handles and switches can give a tired kitchen a facelift.
- Decanting provisions into uniform storage jars looks well-ordered and consistent.
- Focusing on detail often means taking the time to clean and maintain surfaces and finishes properly. It is far easier to clean up as you go along rather than to face a gargantuan task later on.
- Make sure you keep on top of running repairs, such as leaking taps.
- What you do not see is just as important as what is out on view. For example, overloaded sockets and trailing wires indicate a basic planning shortfall.

ABOVE: A MODULAR STORAGE UNIT ON CASTORS SERVES AS ADDITIONAL COUNTER SPACE, WITH ROOM TO DISPLAY DISHES AND STORE COOKBOOKS UNDERNEATH.

RIGHT: A LONG SHELF ON INVISIBLE FIXINGS PROVIDES A PLACE TO PROP A COLLECTION OF FRAMED PICTURES, GIVING A KITCHEN A MORE FURNISHED APPEARANCE.

# Display

People vary in their attitudes to kitchen display. While streamlined kitchens where everything is hidden away can be a little sterile, kitchens where clutter reigns supreme are a muddle to work in. It is fair to say that whatever you leave out in open view should either be in daily use or make some aesthetic contribution to the space as a whole.

- Racks and rails can be used to organize and store basic utensils and pots and pans; open shelving makes a good place to keep condiments, basic ingredients and small appliances that are in regular use.
- A section of wall painted with blackboard paint, where you can chalk up messages and shopping lists, can be a useful way of keeping organized. Alternatively, a noticeboard makes a handy place to pin up reminders, postcards and family snapshots.
- Furnish an eating area in a more relaxed way: a rug under the dining table makes a decorative accent; pictures and framed prints on the wall add interest.
- The most natural displays arise directly out of the kitchen's prime function: platters and dishes heaped with fresh fruit and vegetables – many of which keep much better at room temperature than in the refrigerator – are both appetizing and colourful.

ABOVE: AN ENTIRE WALL PAINTED WITH BLACKBOARD PAINT CAN BE A PLACE TO CHALK UP REMINDERS OR TO KEEP LITTLE FINGERS BUSY.

LEFT: A COLLECTION OF ENAMELLED LADLES AND COLANDERS MAKES A CHEERFUL AND UNASSUMING KITCHEN DISPLAY.

# Kitchen safety

Most accidents happen in the home. You need to pay particular attention to safety if your household includes children or the elderly.

Choose appliances with safety features, such as flame-failure devices on hobs, child-locks and non-tilt shelves in ovens.

- Shorten flexes on small appliances or replace them with curly flexes to prevent children from tugging on them.
- Make sure switches and power points are installed well away from the sink.
- Site cookers and hobs away from windows.
- High-level ovens reduce the risk of children burning themselves on hot oven doors.
- Plan the kitchen so that the distances between the main areas of activity are not too great in order to lessen the risk of dropping hot heavy pans or dishes.
- Fit child locks to any drawer or cupboard that houses sharp utensils, cleansers and other potentially hazardous items.
- Flooring should be as non-slip as possible.
- Clean the floor quickly if you accidently spill oil or grease.
- Keep a small fire extinguisher, fire blanket and first aid box to hand.
- Make sure work surfaces and cooking areas are adequately illuminated.
- Turn pan handles away from the edge of the cooker or hob.
- Worktops should have rounded corners.
- Glazing, particularly large expanses of glazing that can confuse the eye, should be made of toughened safety glass that does not shatter, but crumbles into harmless fragments.

ABOVE: KITCHENS NEED HIGHER LEVELS OF ILLUMINATION THAN ELSEWHERE IN THE HOME. HERE, SMALL INFORMATION LIGHTS ARE INSET INTO THE PLINTH OF FITTED CABINETS.

RIGHT: EYE-LEVEL OVENS MAKE IT EASY TO CHECK FOOD DURING COOKING AND REDUCE THE RISK OF BACK STRAIN WHEN LIFTING OUT HEAVY CASSEROLES.

# Index

# Acknowledgements

The publisher would like to thank Red Cover Picture Library for their kind permission to reproduce the following photographs

6–7 Paul Massey; 10 Paul Ryan-Goff (Architect: Deborah Berke); 11 Winfried Heinze; 12 Tria Giovan (Architect: Lisa Pope Westerman, Domestic Art-Curated Interiors' From the Pages of Paper City' by Holly Moore); 13 Henry Wilson; 16 Winfried Heinze; 17 Alun Callender; 18 James Balston (Architect: MPS); 19 Stuart McIntyre; 20 Johnny Bouchier; 21 Jake Fitzjones (www.martynclarkearchitecture.com); 22 Paul Ryan-Goff (Architects: Olle Rex Architects); 23 Alun Callender; 24 Jake Fitzjones; 25 Jake Fitzjones; 26 Jake Ftizjones; 28 Paul Ryan-Goff; 29 Winfried Heinze; 30 Jake Fitzjones (Neil Lerner Kitchens); 31 Ed Reeve; 32 Winfried Heinze (Architect: Klaus Konig); 33 Alun Callender; 34 Simon Scarboro; 35 Andrew Wood; 36 Christopher Drake; 37 Ken Hayden (Designer: Nigel Pearce); 38 Richard Holt; 39 Dan Duchars; 40 Nial McDiarmid; 41 Chris Tubbs; 42 Jake Fitzjones; 43 Paul Ryan-Goff (Architect: Ken Foreman); 44 Winfried Heinze; 45 Mark York; 46 Steve Dalton; 47 Huntley Hedworth; 48 Practical Pictures (New York Roof Garden, Designer: Halsted Welles); 49 Debi Treloar; 50 Jake Fitzjones; 51 Johnny Bouchier; 54 Winfried Heinze; 55 Helen Miller (Designer: Clare Nash); 56 Douglas Gibb; 57 Chris Tubbs; 58 Henry Wilson; 59 Jake Fitzjones; 60 Douglas Gibb; 61 Jake Fitzjones (Neil Lerner Kitchens); 62 Jake Fitzjones (Architect: Paul Archer); 63 Ken Hayden; 64 Winfried Heinze; 65 Jennifer Cawley; 66 Jake Fitzjones (Architect: Alternative Plans); 67 Paul Ryan-Goff; 68 Jake Fitzjones; 69 Jake Fitzjones (Stylist: Shani Zion, Shop: Diverse); 70 Winfried Heinze (Designer Patricia Jocham, Architect: Klaus Kathan); 71 Mike Daines; 72 Alun Callender; 73 Johnny Bouchier; 74 Johnny Bouchier; 75 Douglas Gibb; 76 Johnny Bouchier; 77 Alun Callender; 78 Evan Skiar; 79 Simon McBride; 80 Paul Massey; 81 Johnny Bouchier; 82 Jake Fitzjones; 83 Henry Wilson; 84 Ed Reeve; 85 Winfried Heinze (Designer: Olaf Mueller-Eckhardt); 86 Paul Ryan-Goff; 87 Simon McBride; 88 Graham Atkins-Hughes; 89 Christopher Drake; 92 Graham Atkins-Hughes; 93 Graham Atkins-Hughes; 94 Dan Duchars; 95 Andrew Wood; 96 Alun Callender; 97 Stuart McIntyre; 98 Henry Wilson; 99 Debi Treloar; 100 Ed Reeve; 101 Brian Harrison; 102 Andrew Wood; 103 Paul Massey; 104 Johnny Bouchier; 105 Chris Tubbs; 106 Ed Reeve; 107 Tria Giovan; 108 Jake Fitzjones; 109 Johnny Bouchier.

Except for the following photograph:
page 2 Winfried Heinze/Conran Octopus

First published in 2010 by Conran Octopus Ltd, a part of Octopus Publishing Group, Endeavour House, 189 Shaftesbury Avenue, London WC2H 8JG www.octopusbooks.co.uk

A Hachette UK Company www.hachette.co.uk

Distributed in the United States and Canada by Octopus Books USA, c/o Hachette Book Group USA, 237 Park Avenue, New York, NY 10017 USA

Text copyright © Conran Octopus Ltd 2010
Design and layout copyright © Conran Octopus Ltd 2010

The right of Terence Conran to be identified as the Author of this work has been asserted by him in accordance with the Copyright, Designs and Patents Act 1988.

British Library Cataloguing-in-Publication Data.
A catalogue record for this book is available from the British Library.

Consultant Editor: Elizabeth Wilhide

Publisher: Lorraine Dickey
Managing Editor: Sybella Marlow
Editor: Bridget Hopkinson

Art Director: Jonathan Christie
Picture Researcher: Liz Boyd
Design Assistant: Mayumi Hashimoto

Production Manager: Katherine Hockley

ISBN: 978 1 84091 549 5
Printed in China